funky chairs

funky chairs

Sit down in style: 25 sensational seats

Catherine Tully

Photography by Graham Rae

southwater

This edition is published by Southwater

Southwater is an imprint of
Anness Publishing Limited
Hermes House
88–89 Blackfriars Road
London SE1 8HA
tel. 020 7401 2077
fax 020 7633 9499

Distributed in the USA by
Anness Publishing Inc.
27 West 20th Street
Suite 504
New York
NY 10011
fax 212 807 6813

Distributed in the UK by
The Manning Partnership
251–253 London Road East
Batheaston
Bath BA1 7RL
tel. 01225 852 727
fax 01225 852 852

Distributed in Australia by
Sandstone Publishing
Unit 1
360 Norton Street
Leichhardt
New South Wales 2040
tel. 02 9560 7888
fax 02 9560 7488

1 3 5 7 9 10 8 6 4 2

Publisher: Joanna Lorenz
Senior Editor: Clare Nicholson
Photographer: Graham Rae
Designer: Caroline Reeves

Previously published as *Chair Dressing*

CONTENTS

INTRODUCTION

Even the most minimal of design schemes includes a chair: everyone needs somewhere to sit! The variety of design possibilities and the practicality and indispensability of chairs mean that spending time, money and energy on them is very worthwhile.

In this book, we have started from the premise that no one has a limitless budget and so most of us have to "make do and mend" for at least part of our furnishing schemes. Also, you may well be faced with an inherited chair that is too good to relegate to the bin and yet not at all in keeping with your modern interior.

As you experiment, you will benefit from the education of your eye. This means you will perceive sculptural shapes and simple, wholesome lines that may be hidden under drab and dingy paintwork or off-putting upholstery and which won't be noticed by the less discerning buyer. Junk-shop finds, sometimes bought for next to nothing, can become individual masterpieces of your own devising, giving your home a wonderful sense of personality and your own style.

Often, chairs need very little more than a new cover to give them a new lease of life, so you don't have to think of sacrificing every weekend for months to take on a worthwhile project. Another bonus is that old chairs are often traditionally upholstered, without foam, and are structurally very sturdy. By renovating, you will often end up with a chair of a far higher quality than any but the most expensive modern equivalent.

DESIGN CLASSICS

Prior to the 1950s, chairs were generally designed following one of the first classic chairs which was called the Windsor. They were invariably made from wood, and they were designed following certain restraints and using classic formulae that had been in use for many decades. However, with the advent of new materials such as plastic and steel, there was a huge surge of new designs which revolutionized chairs. These new designs have now become modernist classics. Do not feel restrained by having to use traditional wooden chairs – the variety of materials used today are very extensive.

Above: This design of this chair has been strongly influenced by the design of the classic Windsor chair.

Above: Half-circle chairs came in every guise from straw to multi-coloured felt.

Above: One of the great designers of the 1950s was Charles Eames who designed stunning fibreglass chairs.

Above: Carl Jacobs designed comfortable and innovative chairs by using cut out designs from plywood.

Left: Houelskou further pushed back the boundaries of chair design, as illustrated by his harp chair.

PAINT EFFECTS

Above: Freehand "painterly" chair; here, after the style of the Spanish artist Miró.

A lick of paint is the quickest way to transform a chair from a derelict shell to an object of baroque opulence or nonchalant charm. If the effect palls after a while or you change your decoration scheme, you can just repaint the chair to give it another lease of life. While painting, you can opt either for a decorative pattern or for a complete, all-over paint effect such as marbling. Sometimes, as in the case of the garden chair, rather than making something that is already old look as good as new, you want a new piece to have a more weathered appearance. This can apply indoors as well as out, but there is a particular charm in garden furniture that looks as though it has stood in its place for many years. The advantages of painting a chair in these circumstances is that a brand new, hard-wearing but possibly rather characterless object can grow into a chair of distinction, with its strength unaffected.

Modern technology means that the colour range available is virtually unlimited, so painting allows you unrivalled opportunities for playing with colour. Remember a few basic principles, though. Pale colours "loom" and make objects look bigger; conversely, the same object painted in a dark colour will look smaller. Complementary colours (red and green, violet and yellow) used together have tremendous impact. For more subtle effects, use different shades of the same colour.

You can buy kits for different paint techniques from good paint or craft shops. For the best results when giving any chair a make over, strip the chair of all its old coats of paint and varnish, so that you have a clean and even surface to work on. For advice on stripping and sanding down, see the basic techniques section at the back of the book. If you use a proprietary chemical paint stripper, it is important to follow the manufacturer's instructions carefully. After you have finished painting, it is also wise to give the chair a coat of varnish to seal and protect it. If you have used a water-based paint, then apply a water-based varnish, but if you have used an oil-based paint, then you should use an oil-based varnish.

Above: A marbled chair; many "stone" effects, such as slate or concrete, would be equally effective.

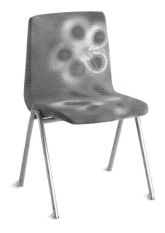

Above: Sprayed vacuum-formed or metal chair, with masked-off portions.

Left: Crackle-glazed garden chair.

FABRIC EFFECTS

Above: A chair covered in lycra, with a distorted pattern; this was originally a swimwear fabric.

There is generally a distinction drawn between fabrics that are intended for soft furnishings and those which are intended for the world of high fashion and the couture house. However, there is no reason why you can't use fabrics for a different purpose from the one for which they were intended and there are many fashion fabrics that will give a magical richness to any upholstery. Colour and trend forecasters now work very closely with both fashion and interior designers. Whereas, in the past, soft furnishings changed very little from season to season, what is available in interiors stores today is as fresh and up to date in style, and as expressive of the mood of the times, as the clothes in boutiques.

Within the book there are several projects on covering chairs with fabric. Do not feel bound to follow the style and look suggested in the project, because the same techniques can be adapted to suit any style of interior. For example, a stunning effect can be created by using velvet instead of a dust sheet for the buttoned chair. Wrap a chair in a large velvet tablecloth and then add buttons in the same or a contrasting colour. You can fold scraps of fabric over self-cover buttons and apply them on the back. With this in mind, always keep your eyes open for large pieces of material, such as old curtains that are no longer being used for their original purpose, because they can always be used as a chair throw. Second-hand shops are good hunting grounds, and many bargains can be found.

Some of the projects described in this book require the use of a sewing machine, but no complicated upholstery techniques are involved. Most have straight edges, and any untidy seams can always be hidden with piping or decorative braid. To keep things simple, we have avoided using fiddly buttonholes or zips; in any case, the tie fastenings we have devised look far more stylish as well as being extremely practical. Glue guns and staple guns are invaluable, as they give quick results. If you are at all nervous about sewing, or do not have a sewing machine, take full advantage of both these and the many non-fraying fabrics available that do not need hemming.

Above: Stool covered in rich purple textured fabric.

Above: Using a dust sheet as a chair cover is a simple and effective way of giving a new lease of life to an old chair. The large buttons are a neat finishing touch.

Above: Seat pad covered in sequins to create a diva-style chair.

INSTANT EMBELLISHMENTS

Above: Chair embellished with seashells and rope.

Great effects can often be achieved by simple techniques. It's worth attempting an easy, very fun look on a spare chair, which can then be a lasting centrepiece in a dull corner of the hall, cloakroom or bathroom. The sorts of ideas shown in these pictures are also really useful as disposable embellishments for a party or a themed dinner. Boldness is the key to success: it can elevate a half-hearted idea into a statement. There are also many more muted embellishments that are intended to blend subtly into the existing interior, for example tassels. These are available in a wide range of colours, sizes and materials, from bright pink plastic to luxurious-looking soft silken yarns, so it is easy to find tassels to suit every style. On a wooden chair, they can be hung from the back struts or, for a soft armchair, they can be sewn on to the front of the arms. Matching trimmings and braids are also a quick and simple way of drawing attention away from worn patches in chairs and for covering up blemishes.

Don't, however, feel that you have to restrict yourself to what is available in your nearest department store or haberdasher's. DIY stores and garden centres are equally good sources of materials and offer a range that will set fire to your imagination: rope, garden twine, raffia, even chains and electrician's wire could all be used. A glue gun is a good investment, also.

In a country location, an effective party idea for decorating a chair is to tie bunches of dried flowers or herbs with string or decorative ribbon and hang them from the back of the chair. For a more rustic look, use straw, dyed raffia or even twine. At Christmas, you could substitute bunches of holly tied with festive red or tartan ribbon.

Another very simple way of transforming a straight-back chair is to glue flat pearly buttons in a straight line up the back struts and around the seat edge. This looks particularly effective on a dark wooden chair. On a limed chair, cockle shells and tiny starfish would give a seaside air.

Above: Chair "flocked" with string.

Above: Silk tassel tied around a chair leg.

Above: Chair decorated with studs.

ALTERNATIVE CHAIRS

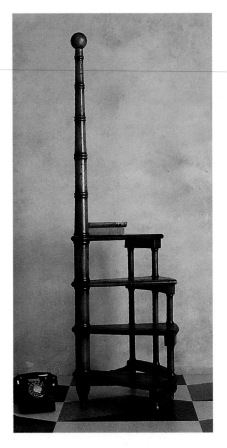

Above: This old-fashioned library step ladder would make a wonderful chair while also fulfilling its original function.

How often have you seen gamine Audrey Hepburn or glamorous Grace Kelly perched attractively on library steps reading a book, or curled on a trunk or packing case eating toast? We often try to emulate the glamour of old films and their stars when we are considering new furnishings, but we forget that they also made everyday objects glamorous by association.

Even if you don't aspire to the celluloid style of Hollywood in its heyday, you can still take a tip from these old films: there are many objects that were never intended to be used as chairs but which can provide stylish seating and, as well as looking good, they retain their original usefulness as well!

Who has not found themselves in the potentially embarrassing situation of having to improvise seating on those infuriating occasions when we find we have invited too many people to lunch or friends unexpectedly turn up when we are already entertaining others. As usual, it is children who usually have the brightest ideas in such circumstances, since most will sit on anything. (Who does not remember, as a child, being made to sit on the arm of a settee, on a footstool or just on a cushion on the floor?) A coffee table, provided it is strong enough, can be transformed into a useful stool simply by putting a few cushions on it, and you can always disguise it further with an attractive throw. If it is less than solid, use it for putting your feet up. Old car seats are ideal for outdoor summer parties and, if they recline, all you need do is spread a large beach towel over them to make splendid improvised sun loungers.

A sense of humour is the watchword here: no one should expect the ultimate in comfort, but with a little imagination, it is not difficult to find objects that could be turned into acceptable seating at a moment's notice. Some wastepaper baskets are surprisingly sturdy when up-ended, if on the low side. If you need to seat extra people at a table, a broad plank between two stools would make a decent pew (provided the heavier guests sat at the ends), and a few cushions would provide comfort.

Above: Although metal trunks do not make practical suitcases, they are useful if you live in a small flat, because they can double up as a seat and a storage chest.

Above: Children's toys can be used as temporary seats.

Above: If you are throwing a party and you are short of seats, why not put the crates the wine came in to good use as alternative chairs?

Above: This churn is another idea for a seat which could also be used for storage.

FABRIC-SWATHED CHAIR

This effect is stylish and practical and yet needs no sewing skills. None of the usual difficulties caused by the need for washing of fitted covers apply, so you can capitalize on the sheer drama that is created by brilliant white. A generous quantity of fabric is the only essential; this project uses a king-size, pure cotton sheet, which is ready-hemmed, but you can use any wide, preferably washable, fabric that is soft enough to knot and tie. Why not consider this as a stunning addition to your Christmas scheme, by wrapping the dining chairs in red silk?

YOU WILL NEED

♦ chair

♦ fabric

♦ sewing machine, if necessary

1 You need at least twice, and preferably three times, as much fabric as the width of your chair. Hem the fabric, if necessary. Throw the fabric over the chair and centre it.

2 Tuck fabric down the back behind the seat of the chair. If the chair has arms, do this all around the seat, so that the cover doesn't pull when you sit on the chair.

3 Sweep the fabric round to the back of the chair.

4 Tie a knot, making sure that the fabric is an even length on both sides and that you have attractive folds and drapes at the sides. Try to tie the knot confidently in one go: otherwise the fabric can look tortured and may be crumpled. Remember that the fabric should cascade down from the knot.

ASTROTURF CHAIR

Classic conservatory chairs are usually made of expensive hardwood and are often boring in design. For a truly modern garden room, therefore, why not jazz up a cheap fifties metal chair with astroturf, available from garden centres and DIY stores, and some artificial flowers – usually considered kitsch, their use is definitely tongue-in-cheek here. The chair would also be ideal for a garden party.

YOU WILL NEED

- ♦ metal chair
- ♦ screwdriver
- ♦ fine- and coarse- grade astroturf
- ♦ staple gun
- ♦ ruler
- ♦ craft knife
- ♦ glue gun
- ♦ artificial flowers

1 Unscrew the seat pad and cut a piece of fine-grade astroturf to cover it. Staple it in place.

2 Measure and cut strips of a coarser grade of astroturf and attach to the seat with a glue gun.

3 Cut two matching pieces of coarse astroturf to fit over the central back struts. Glue the artificial flowers to the front piece.

4 Fix both pieces over the struts with a glue gun.

DIRECTOR'S CHAIR IN KELIM FABRIC

Director's chairs are inexpensive, but because they are made of cloth are very comfortable. Plain canvas seats are the norm but by customizing you can create a fun, very chic effect. Kelim fabric is very hard-wearing and has beautiful muted colours, but any fabric that is strong and without too much "give" can be used, such as tapestry, hessian, sacking or carpet. For even more character, stain the frame to match the muted tones of the kelim.

YOU WILL NEED

♦ director's chair
♦ wood stain and paintbrush (optional)
♦ kelim carpet or fabric
♦ dressmaker's pins
♦ scissors
♦ large darning or upholstery needle
♦ strong darning wool
♦ packet of chrome poppers (at least 6)
♦ hammer

1 Remove the old seat and back. Stain the wood of the chair, if you want.

2 Choose the most decorative parts of the kelim and pin the old fabric to it as a pattern. Carefully cut out new seat and back pieces.

3 Thread the needle with the wool and neatly blanket stitch the edges to bind them.

4 Fold over the edges of the back and fasten with chrome poppers, then slip over the uprights. Slot the seat back into position and secure firmly.

SLIP-COVERED DIRECTOR'S CHAIR

Completely draped in a slip cover, a director's chair loses its functional character and takes on the role of an armchair. Avoid complicated fitting by cutting a tabard- type slip cover, based on squares and rectangles and simply tied together. You can then put the cover straight on to the chair without ironing, since it can be removed and stored flat when the chair is folded away.

YOU WILL NEED

♦ director's chair
♦ measuring tape
♦ 2.5m/2¹/₂yd of 137cm/54in fabric
♦ fabric marker
♦ set square and ruler
♦ scissors
♦ dressmaker's pins
♦ sewing machine and matching thread
♦ iron

1 With the chair assembled, measure: (a) from floor to top edge of back; (b) from top edge of back to back of seat; (c) length of seat; (d) width of seat; (e) from centre of wooden armrest to inside base of seat; (f) from centre of armrest to floor; (g) from front edge of seat to floor.

2 Measure and draw the pattern pieces directly on to the fabric, with a seam allowance all round each piece. Cut out, then pin, tack and sew the pieces together following the diagram at the back of the book.

3 Mark and cut strips of fabric to make ties of a finished size of about 2.5cm/1in wide and 40cm/16in long. Put right sides together and sew the long edges together. Then turn them out and slip stitch the ends.

4 Assemble the tabard as a cross (see diagram). Slip the finished cover over the chair and knot the ties firmly.

GUSTAVIAN CHAIR

In contrast to the stern and imposing mahogany of tradition, pretty Gustavian painted chairs have given a new lightness and elegance to dining-room furniture. They are very expensive, however, because few are available outside Scandinavia, where they originated. Create your own by hunting for a wooden chair of the classic shape and then paint it. The chair should have a padded seat and pretty outlines, if possible, and enough space on the back rest for a motif. The traditional Scandinavian colours for painted chairs were greys, dark blues, aquamarine, honey yellow and red, as well as white, of course. Muted shades and washed effects are of the essence; this is what keeps the look light and airy.

YOU WILL NEED

- ◆ classic wooden chair
- ◆ medium- and fine-grade sandpaper
- ◆ household paintbrush
- ◆ white, blue and black emulsion paint
- ◆ fine and medium paintbrushes
- ◆ monogram motif
- ◆ tracing paper
- ◆ soft and hard pencils
- ◆ masking tape
- ◆ clear matt varnish
- ◆ typeface or script samples (e.g. from a calligraphy book)
- ◆ large sheet of paper
- ◆ scissors
- ◆ 1m/1yd of 137cm/54in (or twice seat-cover width) white cotton fabric
- ◆ indelible laundry or fabric marker
- ◆ staple gun
- ◆ needle and matching thread
- ◆ gold and silver spray paint

1 Lightly sand the chair with medium-grade sandpaper, to make a key for the paintwork.

2 Paint the chair with an undercoat of white emulsion.

3 Using the fine paintbrush, carefully outline the shape of the back of the chair in blue-grey emulsion. Add similar detailing to the seat and legs. Leave to dry.

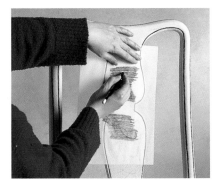

4 Trace your chosen letters and scrolls. Turn the tracing paper over, and rub all over the back with the soft pencil. Turn it over, position it on the chair back and tape it in place. Go over the outlines with a hard pencil to transfer them to the chair.

5 Fill in the outlines in blue-grey with the medium paintbrush. Be confident! Refer to your original reference for where the brush strokes should be thicker. Allow to dry. Apply a coat of matt varnish (water-based varnishes have very short drying times).

6 Cut a piece of paper roughly the size of the chair seat pad, to give you an idea of the area to which you need to apply lettering. Photocopy type alphabets or sections of script, enlarging them, if necessary.

7 Cut up the script and arrange the pieces on the paper.

8 Put the paper against a brightly lit window, and smooth the cloth over the design. Fix to the glass with masking tape. Using the fabric marker, trace over the letters. ➞

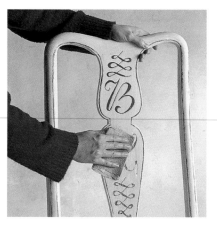

9 Cover the seat pad with the fabric, securing it on the back with staples. Take a second piece of fabric, just smaller than the back of the seat, turn under the edges and sew in place to cover the staples.

11 Replace the seat pad in the chair. Lightly sand the paint with fine-grade sandpaper, to give it a charming, slightly aged effect.

10 Lightly spray over the whole seat with gold paint. Repeat with silver.

Right: The softly coloured wood is usually teamed with a simple checked or striped seat cover, but we have chosen a more unusual and regal approach, using a script or type as inspiration. You can adapt this idea, for example using musical notes and symbols for a music-room chair.

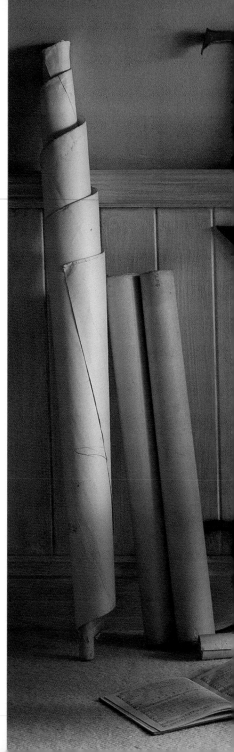

COMIC-STRIP CHAIR

This montage idea has bags of impact and could be adapted to many different themes. Here, we have chosen comic-strip characters to create a chair that would be welcome in the coolest teenager's bedroom. For a prettier look, brighten a conservatory chair with a montage made from seed packets, catalogues or gardening magazines, or a kitchen chair with canned fruit labels. The seat cover could use any brightly coloured logo or graphic cut from fabric, or make use of a favourite image by taking a picture to a high street shop that transfers pictures on to T-shirts. Try to choose images that suit the scale of the chair or, for more fun, stick masses of pictures of tiny doll's chairs on a large chair, for example, or a huge pair of boots on a tiny shoe-cleaning stool.

YOU WILL NEED

- ♦ wooden-framed chair
- ♦ medium-grade sandpaper
- ♦ scissors
- ♦ paper motifs
- ♦ wallpaper paste
- ♦ paintbrushes
- ♦ clear gloss varnish or aerosol gloss varnish
- ♦ blue stretchy fabric
- ♦ staple gun
- ♦ fabric logo (optional)
- ♦ fabric adhesive (optional)

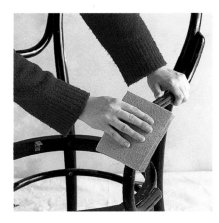

2 Sand the chair lightly all over, to provide a key for the paste.

1 Remove the seat from the chair.

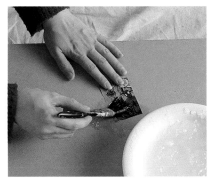

3 Cut out the motifs carefully with sharp-pointed scissors. Apply paste carefully all over the back of the motifs. Leave until tacky.

4 Brush wallpaper paste over the chair frame, then apply the motifs to the chair, using a brush to prevent tearing them while they are wet.

5 Repeat until you have covered the whole chair, liberally applying wallpaper paste. Leave to dry.

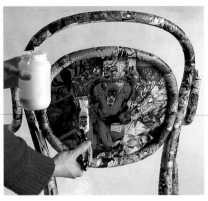

6 Apply a coat of varnish to protect the chair.

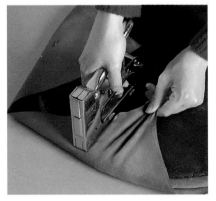

7 For the seat cushion, stretch the fabric over the cushion and staple it in place. Pull the fabric taut as you work round the cushion.

8 If you wish to decorate the seat further, find a logo or graphic to go in the centre. Apply fabric adhesive to the back and allow it to become tacky.

9 Position and apply the logo to the seat cushion, pressing it down firmly until the glue has taken hold. Replace the cushion in the chair.

ESCHER'S DECKCHAIR

Deckchairs are cheap and widely available in several styles, with variations on the original design, such as foot rests and small canopies. The slings are nearly always canvas, which can be bought from high street stores in a variety of brightly coloured plains and stripes. Deckchair canvas is the correct width and comes with ready-sealed edges. To give an old chair a new lease of life, use lots of oversized stencils in a repeat pattern or turn checks into a "three-dimensional" puzzle, as here. This design is based on work by the artist Escher and is made from a positive (white) motif and a negative (black) motif combined.

YOU WILL NEED
- deckchair
- deckchair canvas
- scissors
- spray adhesive
- high-density foam
- self-healing cutting mat
- craft knife
- ruler or set square
- coloured tape
- pencil
- paintbrush
- black and white fabric paints
- needle and matching thread

1 Remove the old sling, making a note of how it was fastened so that you can fasten it up in the same way later.

2 Using the old cover as a pattern, cut out the new fabric, allowing for seams along the top and bottom edges.

3 To make the two stamps for printing, photocopy the motifs from the back of the book to the desired size. Stick to the foam with spray adhesive. Cut round the design with the craft knife.

33

4 Using the knife, chip away the zigzag shape between the dotted lines to leave two elements of the design standing proud. Remove all the foam which isn't part of the "negative" design. It is helpful to mark the backs of the stamps with tape, to indicate which colour paint is used with which stamp.

6 Using a ruler and pencil, draw parallel lines lengthways on the canvas, the distance between them equalling the full width of the design when the two stamps are put together (see step 9).

8 Applying light, even pressure, stamp the black design regularly within the grid lines.

9 Repeat with the white design. When dry, hem the top and bottom edges of the canvas, then fasten to the chair frame.

5 Repeat steps 3 and 4 to make the "positive" stamp.

7 Apply the black paint to the raised portion of one of the stamps.

Opposite: When stamping, do not apply too much paint to the stamp.

DINING CHAIR WITH LACING

Transform a run-of-the-mill chair into a modern piece with the added bonus of increased comfort at the dining table and the opportunity to introduce more dramatic colours tastefully. These covers can be permanent or changed at whim. Any bright canvas fabric is suitable; cotton duck, which is very reasonably priced, has been used here. The fabric must have a little body or you will need to add a backing fabric. Ticking, canvas, linen or duck are all hard-wearing and give a sufficiently sculptural shape.

As an alternative to the lacing and eyelets, use self-cover buttons with cord or loops or, for the more adventurous and skilled, buttonholes. Loops and toggles or frogging give a military look, especially with a bright scarlet fabric.

YOU WILL NEED

♦ dining chair

♦ measuring tape

♦ rubberized horse hair or foam
(to fit the back of the chair)

♦ scissors

♦ tape for ties

♦ thin wadding (to fit the back of the chair)

♦ upholstery tacks

♦ felt-tipped pen

♦ tissue or pattern-cutting paper

♦ 3m/3yd of 130cm/50in wide cotton duck

♦ dressmaker's pins

♦ sewing machine and matching thread

♦ iron

♦ safety pins

♦ fabric marker

♦ hole-punching tool

♦ 8 eyelets

♦ eyelet pliers

♦ hammer

♦ 3m/3yd cotton tape

1 Measure the chair back for the size of the foam backing or rubberized horse hair. Cut the backing to size and attach it to the chair back with ties at the top and bottom.

2 Cover the foam or horse hair loosely with thin wadding, securing with tacks.

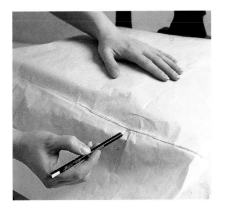

3 Lay the paper on the seat and draw round it to make a pattern, adding a seam allowance. Make a pattern for the front of the seat back.

5 For the skirt, measure the two sides and front of the seat, then add 30cm/12in for each of the four box pleats. Add 4cm/1½in to the depth as a seam allowance. Make a pattern.

7 Stitch the front panel to the top of the seat panel with the right sides together. Trim and press open all the seams as you go.

4 Decide how deep you would like the skirt to be, then work out the dimensions for the back. The back panel incorporates a box pleat to allow easy removal (see the diagram at the back of the book). Draw a pattern.

6 Lay the patterns on your material and cut out each piece. Take the back panel and pin, then stitch the central box pleat down to about 4cm/1½in from the top of the seat and press it.

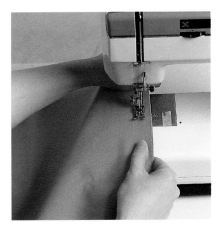

8 Stitch the front panel to the back at the top and sides.

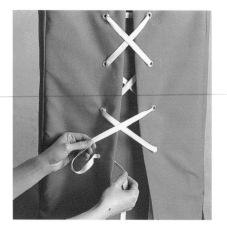

9 Hem the bottom edge of the skirt. Fold and pin the box pleats so they fall in the corners of the seat. Machine stitch the seat and skirt in place along the top edges.

11 Remove the cover. Using a hole-punching tool, make holes for the eyelets.

13 Put the cover on the chair and lace up the back with tapes.

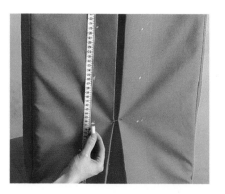

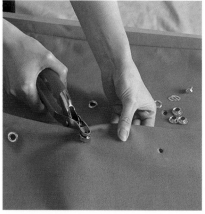

10 Put the cover on the seat, close the back pleat with safety pins and mark where the eyelets are to be with a fabric marker.

12 Following the manufacturer's instructions, attach the eyelets.

Opposite: For a modern room, each chair could be covered in a different jewel colour or beautiful natural weaves and linen could be used for a restful and calm room.

STOOL WITH WOOD MOULDINGS

This is a very simple and yet effective look, which doesn't involve any complicated techniques. The wood mouldings are available in a considerable range from your local timber merchant or hardware store and are intended for embellishing doors and panelling. However, they also give instant texture to otherwise plain objects, lending them unexpected style.

YOU WILL NEED

- ♦ wooden stool
- ♦ white undercoat paint, if necessary
- ♦ paintbrushes
- ♦ ruler
- ♦ pencil
- ♦ wooden mouldings
- ♦ glue gun
- ♦ oil-based brown paint, mixed with 2 parts matt glaze (scumble)
- ♦ creamy white oil paint
- ♦ dry brush

1 If your stool is already painted in strong colours, paint it white to give a neutral base colour.

2 Draw a central grid in pencil on the sides of the stool and decide on the positioning of the mouldings. Stick them on to the surface.

3 Using the brown glaze and working continuously in one direction (to simulate the grain of the wood), paint the whole stool.

4 Using a pale wash of cream, paint over the mouldings to highlight them. Remove some of the glaze while still wet with a dry brush, to give the stool a limed appearance.

JEWEL-BRIGHT RUBBER CHAIR

Many elegantly shaped armchairs are disguised beneath layers of ugly orange varnish and dowdy fabrics. Once the covers are removed, however, these chairs can be transformed instantly into desirable objects. Stretchy fabrics make it easier to achieve a professional finish, but any upholstery fabric is suitable.

YOU WILL NEED

♦ armchair
♦ medium-grade sandpaper
♦ clear wax or silicone polish
♦ rubber fabric
♦ scissors
♦ staple gun
♦ rubber adhesive
♦ paintbrush
♦ hammer
♦ upholstery tacks
♦ thick artist's card

1 Remove all the old covers. Sand the varnish from the frame. Seal with clear wax or silicone polish.

2 Using the existing cover pieces as patterns, cut the fabric to the size of the back rest, with a generous allowance to turn to the back surface. Stretch it over the back rest until it is hand-tight and staple it in place. Secure, in order, the top, bottom and sides, with one or two staples in the centre, before applying lines of staples to keep the fabric taut.

3 Cut a piece of fabric to fit the back surface of the back rest and apply rubber adhesive to the fabric and the chair. Allow to become tacky and apply the fabric, covering the staples and the turned-over edges of the first layer. Hammer a tack into each corner.

4 For the cushion, trace its shape on to the card. Cut out and staple to the cushion. Wrap the fabric around the cushion and staple to the card. Attach a layer of fabric to the underside of the cushion, following step 3 and using rubber adhesive.

GILDED CHAIR

Many a beautiful antique bentwood chair is relegated to the attic or the back of the shop because its cane seat has become worn and tatty or damaged. Re-caning is expensive and it is hard to find skilled craftsmen to do it; it often seems easier and cheaper to buy a new chair. This is a terrible shame because a bentwood chair can become the star of a room, with some effort but very little extra expense, by setting in a solid seat. Once the lightness of the cane has been removed, the chair looks better with the more dramatic foil of gold leaf decoration, or at least a textured paint finish, than left as solid black or stained wood. A good art shop can supply the correct type of size, gold leaf and varnish for your needs. You could also experiment with silver leaf.

1 If the seat needs repairing, cut away the cane with a sharp craft knife.

2 Using a screwdriver or bradawl, pick out the remaining strands of cane. To make the corner blocks which will support the new seat, hold the pieces of wood inside each corner, mark the shape of the corners on the wood and then cut the pieces to shape.

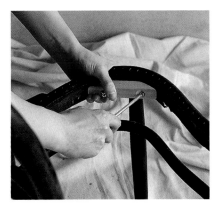

3 Hold a corner block in position and drill through it into the chair. Screw the block into position. Repeat for all four corners.

5 Tape the template to the plywood and draw around it. Cut around the pencil line (a timber merchant can do this for you if do not have a jigsaw).

7 Prepare the chair for gilding by sanding all the surfaces lightly. Roughening the wood helps the size to adhere.

4 Lay the paper over the seat and trace around the shape. Cut out around the shape to create the template.

6 Sand the edges of the wooden seat to fit and drop it into place.

8 Paint the chair with size and allow it to dry. Follow the manufacturer's recommendations.

9 Holding the gold leaf by the backing paper, lay a sheet on the chair.

10 With a clean, dry brush, rub the gold leaf on to the chair. Continue until the chair is covered. It is very important that both the brush and your hands are clean and dry.

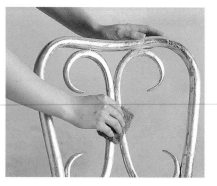

11 Rub the chair with a clean, dry cloth, to remove any loose flakes.

12 Finally, to protect the gold leaf, seal the whole chair with varnish.

Right: This treatment could be used on any chair that has graceful lines and surface areas which are not too large. If you want to treat a chair with a wooden back and seat in this way, add more charm by drilling patterns such as heart shapes.

FIFTIES CHAIR

Covered in Nova suede, this hard-backed chair has a split personality: a kitsch fifties dining chair by day and a theatrical throne in the evening. Throws are often used to cover easy chairs but the limitless possibilities of using them to add drama to a hard chair, totally changing its appearance, are often overlooked. Another advantage is that you can knot throws and tie them on to the uprights of a hard-backed chair and extras such as tassels or bindings can easily be incorporated. Any fabric that is wide enough is suitable, but squashy fabrics, such as suede or velvet, are particularly stylish. Practicality is not an issue, because the covers can be whisked off to reveal the practical chair underneath.

YOU WILL NEED
- ♦ hard-backed chair
- ♦ large piece of plush fabric, for example, Nova suede
- ♦ tassels and bindings (optional)

1 Drape the fabric over the chair, making sure it touches the ground at the front.

2 Take up some excess fabric from the back and form a knot over both chair pegs at the back of the chair.

3 For further embellishment, secure the corners with tassels or bindings.

ROPE-BOUND CHAIR

Colonial-style and veranda chairs have gained considerable popularity recently but, sadly, originals are extremely difficult to find. This is a good technique for a chair whose character would be lost if it were painted or stripped and yet which needs some form of embellishment. Natural trimmings, such as twine, rope or hessian tape, can be expensive, as you will need about 80 metres (90 yards). Look out for less expensive forms of the same product, such as the sash cord used here. You could also use garden twine, rope, washing line or builder's scrim.

YOU WILL NEED

♦ old chair
♦ 6 to 8 x 12m/12yd bales of sash cord
♦ glue gun

1 Starting at the back of the chair, secure the end of the rope with a small amount of glue from the gun.

2 Begin wrapping the chair according to your design.

3 You can use two lengths at a time for the arms, starting with a slip knot.

4 When you reach the end of the length, secure it by tucking it in at the back of the chair and then glue.

SPACE-AGE CHAIRS

For an overdose of the fantastic, create some space-age simplicity and make a statement in your bathroom or kitchen that can't be ignored. Vacuum-formed chairs appeared in vast numbers in our schools and offices, as part of the sixties space-craze. A twenty-first-century update can be given to these forgotten and often discarded chairs by adding yet more space-age technology: shiny silver space blankets, used as emergency blankets. These are easily available from most camping shops and their silver appeal is unsurpassed. Vacuum-formed chairs themselves are the classics of their time and crying out for a facelift. If you don't want silver, a coat of hot pink car spray paint with lime-green legs will give them a lift.

YOU WILL NEED

- ◆ 2 plastic chairs
- ◆ silver car spray paint
- ◆ PVA glue
- ◆ paintbrush
- ◆ 1m/1yd thin wadding
- ◆ 1m/1yd of 137cm/54in iridescent lycra fabric
- ◆ needle and strong thread
- ◆ scissors
- ◆ 4 ping-pong balls
- ◆ craft knife
- ◆ space mat
- ◆ chinagraph pencil
- ◆ space blanket
- ◆ masking tape
- ◆ glue gun
- ◆ 50cm/20in extruded foam pipe

1 Spray the legs of the chairs silver. Apply a coat of PVA glue to the top and underneath of the first chair and stick on the wadding.

2 Stretch the lycra tautly over the chair. Gather the fabric at the back and stitch it in place. Trim off excess fabric and turn and tack to neaten the back. Cut holes in the ping-pong balls and insert a leg into each one.

3 To line the circular hole in the second chair, use the chinagraph pencil to draw the outline of the hole on the underside of the space mat.

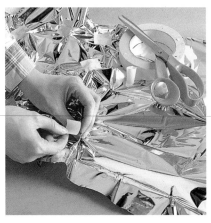

4 With a craft knife, cut a small circle from the centre of the outline and then make straight cuts from the inner to the outer circle.

6 Prepare ruched panels from the space blanket for the sides, and to wrap over the edges of the chair. Hold the ruching in position with masking tape.

8 Hide the join with a strip of folded space mat as "piping", applied with the glue gun.

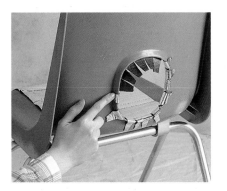

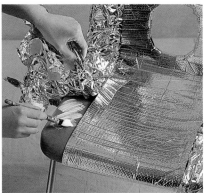

5 Apply PVA glue to the back of the chair and press the cut sections firmly in place. Once the circle has been centred and the glue is tacky, apply the space mat as a continuous strip.

7 Coat the edges of the chair with PVA glue. Secure the ruched sections to the chair, pressing lightly on to the glued areas.

9 Cover the extruded foam pipe with strips of space blanket. Glue it round the hole in the chair, as a cushion.

MINIMALIST OFFICE CHAIR

Sleek, minimalist beech and chrome chairs abound in interiors magazines. However, these classically simple objects have gained price tags to match, which makes renovating old chairs a delightfully rewarding proposition.

Most second-hand office-supply shops and bric-à-brac shops have a host of tatty typist's chairs, often with torn upholstery or in ghastly colours. Look more closely; you never know what interesting features lurk beneath that grime. Look for a good shape. Has it any curves to the seat and back rest? Does the seat mechanism work? Are the chair legs and pedestal made of metal? Don't be drawn to a more modern chair that appears in a better state but has plastic-coated legs; metal legs look far better when renovated.

YOU WILL NEED

- old typist's chair
- scissors
- screwdriver or bradawl
- pliers
- industrial rubber gloves
- chemical paint stripper
- 2.5–5cm/1–2in brush
- wire wool
- medium-grade sandpaper
- all-in-one stain and varnish
- hammer
- "domes of silence"
- chrome or metal polish
- soft, dry cloth

2 Remove the fabric and upholstery staples from the back and underside of the chair. Use the screwdriver or bradawl for getting into tricky places and the pliers to pull out the staples.

1 Start by cutting off excess fabric and foam. You need strong scissors; ones with large plastic handles, like the ones pictured, will not hurt your hands.

3 Remove the castors and any other loose parts, to prevent them from being damaged by the paint stripper.

4 Wearing the protective gloves, brush the paint stripper on to the metal chair frame. Leave for 5 minutes (or as long as the manufacturer recommends) and then wash off with wire wool and soapy water. Repeat until all the paint has been removed.

5 Having removed the seat and back, make sure the surfaces are free of nails and staples. Sand the surfaces and edges of the seat and back until they are smooth and clean.

6 Seal the wood with all-in-one stain and varnish, and leave to dry.

7 Reattach the seat, back and castors. Use "domes of silence" to cover any sharp bolts that might rip your clothes. Finally, shine up the metal and chrome with the polish and a soft, dry cloth.

Right: This renovated office chair has all the style of today's favoured beech and chrome chairs at a fraction of the price.

PULL-DOWN STOOL

Restricted space in flats is common; you need to use every inch and it's not easy to fit in extra seating, for example, by the phone in the hall. Folding chairs are an obvious solution, but the problem still arises of where to store them. A practical answer is to make use of the clever folding brackets and hinges available from DIY stores. These are often used for tables and shelves but, because of their load-bearing ability, can easily be adapted for stools.

Instead of a solid piece of MDF, you could could use dowel decking, such as is used in bathrooms. It is most important that the stool is fitted to a masonry wall and not to a partition wall; always check the manufacturer's recommendations for fitting the right kind of screws and plugs.

YOU WILL NEED

- ♦ pair of folding brackets with screws
- ♦ silver spray paint
- ♦ medium-density fibreboard (MDF)
- ♦ saw
- ♦ pencil
- ♦ ruler
- ♦ pair of compasses or circular templates in three sizes
- ♦ clamp
- ♦ drill with wood and masonry bits
- ♦ jigsaw (optional)
- ♦ medium-grade sandpaper
- ♦ paintbrushes
- ♦ yellow paint
- ♦ clear varnish or lacquer
- ♦ screwdriver
- ♦ 2 long screws and wall plugs
- ♦ spirit level

1 Spray the brackets silver.

2 Cut the MDF to the right size for the seat (30–45–20cm/12–18–8in is normal). Draw a line down the centre of the seat.

3 Place the brackets on the seat and mark their position in pencil.

4 With the compasses, draw three circles of increasing size. Alternatively, find three circular objects of suitable sizes to use as templates.

5 Holding the seat firmly clamped to the work bench, drill a ring of holes just inside the pencil marks; this will allow you to cut out the circles with a jigsaw. If you are not confident with a jigsaw, take the seat to a hardware store or timber merchant who will cut the holes for you.

6 Sand the holes to a smooth finish, both inside and on the top and bottom.

7 Sand off any pencil marks or fingerprints, to prepare the surfaces for painting.

8 Paint the inside of the holes yellow to highlight them.

9 Seal the seat with clear lacquer or varnish (a spray type will give a smooth finish).

10 Screw the brackets to the seat.

11 Hold the seat against the wall (remember, it must be a masonry wall) and mark the position of the first hole with a pencil.

13 Level the seat using a spirit level and mark the position for the second hole on the wall. Drill the hole, insert the plug and screw the other side of the seat to the wall.

12 Drill the hole using the masonry bit. Insert the wall plug and screw the seat loosely to the wall.

14 Check that the stool folds neatly against the wall.

Right: The perfect seat for a small flat.

SHEER FABRIC-COVERED CHAIR

A beautiful chair with wonderful curved legs, a ladder back and cane seat might not seem to need further treatment; yet sometimes, for a change, or for a special occasion, such as a wedding party or a Valentine's Day dinner, you might want to decorate a chair without masking its integral beauty. A wistful, romantic appeal can be given by swathing the chair in translucent fabric to give it a softness which looks very special. The transparent fabric could be coloured or one of the metallic fabrics in gold or silver, so long as the bones of the chair show through. Tie the sash that takes up the extra fabric in a knot or a big, soft bow and leave it either at the back or on the seat, like a cushion.

YOU WILL NEED

♦ wooden chair

♦ tissue or pattern-cutting paper

♦ pencil

♦ dressmaker's pins

♦ 3m/3yd of 137cm/54in transparent silk, voile or organza

♦ fabric marker

♦ dressmaker's scissors

♦ measuring tape

♦ sewing machine, matching thread and iron

1 On the paper, carefully trace the shape of the back rest of the chair. Use this as a template for cutting the back and front of the back rest cover, adding 2cm/¾in all round for seams. Pin the template to the fabric, draw round it and cut out the pieces.

2 Trace the shape of the seat in the same way. Don't worry too much about getting an exact fit; the sash will take up any fullness. Transfer on to the fabric, adding 2cm/¾in all round for seam allowances.

3 Measure from the edge of the seat to the floor, for the depth of the skirt and again add at least 2cm/¾in for a seam allowance. ➤

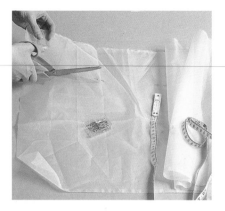

4 For the width of the skirt, add 120cm/48in to the circumference of the chair seat, to allow for the corner box pleats. Cut this as one continuous panel. For the sash, allow a 2m/2yd length of 40cm/16in wide fabric.

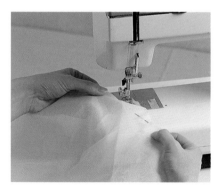

5 Stitch the bottom of the front back rest panel to the top of the seat panel with right sides together. Press open all the seams as you go.

6 With right sides together, stitch the front back rest panel to the back.

7 Hem the bottom edge of the skirt. Fold, press and pin the pleats, positioning them at the corners. Stitch along the top edge of the skirt panel, to hold the pleats in position. Stitch the skirt to the seat panel at the sides and front and to the back panel at the back, positioning the pleats at the corners.

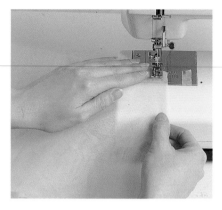

8 Fold the sash in half lengthways, right sides together, and stitch up the long seam and one short seam. Turn the sash right sides out and slip-stitch the open end. Tie the sash round the chair.

PRETTY KITCHEN CHAIR

Introduce pretty Provençal checks and stripes to the kitchen with soft furnishings; many kitchen chairs have detachable pads or padded seats and the informality of the kitchen perfectly suits a jumble of frills, ties and prints.

Consider the colours and patterns of your tablecloths and then, using bright colours, simple ginghams or stripes, mix and match. As an alternative, smart ticking stripes or pale pastels in sugar-almond colours would give this homely chair a more sophisticated air, which might also be more soothing. Frills or box pleats, ties and long ribbons, skirts floating out at jaunty angles or extending to the floor: the changes you can ring are endless.

YOU WILL NEED
- ◆ kitchen chair
- ◆ tissue or pattern-cutting paper
- ◆ pencil
- ◆ thin foam
- ◆ scissors
- ◆ 3m/3yd of 137cm/54in fabric
- ◆ fabric marker
- ◆ measuring tape
- ◆ ruler or set square
- ◆ dressmaker's pins
- ◆ sewing maching, matching thread and iron
- ◆ ribbons or ties (optional)

1 Using the thin paper, draw the shape of the chair seat and cut this out of foam, to form a cushion.

2 On the wrong side of the fabric, draw the cushion shape again, adding a 2cm/³⁄₄in seam allowance.

3 Measure the depth and the circumference of the foam. ⟶

4 Cut a bias strip of fabric to these measurements, with a 4cm/1½in seam allowance all round.

5 Attach the strip to the seat cover, by pinning and machine stitching the pieces together all round the edge, with right sides together.

6 Decide how deep you want the skirt to be. The length is three times the circumference of the seat. From straight-grain fabric, cut one continuous panel or join two together.

7 Hem the bottom edge and the two ends of the panel. Fold, pin and press the fabric into box pleats. When pleated, the skirt should be the same length as the sides and front of the cushion pad. Sew along the top edge, to secure the pleats. Attach the pleats to the bias-cut strip of the chair cover, with right sides together. Leave the back edge of the chair cover free of pleats but turn up the hem allowance on the bias strip, to neaten the edge.

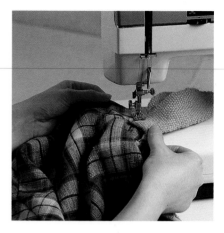

8 Stitch ribbons or tapes to the unfrilled edge and tie them around the back rest, to hold the cover in place. Alternatively cut ties from leftover fabric. Machine stitch them with right sides together, leaving a small gap. Trim the seam allowances and clip the corners, turn them right side out through the gap and slip-stitch the gap closed. Attach the self-ties as for ribbons.

Opposite: There are really no limits to the variations on this style of seat cover: by changing the fabric, colour, style of skirt and way of tying, you can move from cottagey to ethnic, from minimal to intricate, from neutral to eye-catchingly dramatic.

ROBOT CHAIR

A simple chair may not suit a dramatic paint treatment but you can add to basic chairs to create more height or add drama with a ladder-back effect. The easiest addition to use is already turned dowel, available from builders' merchants and DIY shops, which should be the thickness of your drill bit. If you are prepared for extra work in drilling out larger holes, all kinds of struts could be used, including twisted and carved pieces, as used for shelving or balustrades. Decorating the chair with computer-age motifs in fluorescent paint adds further impact.

YOU WILL NEED

- ladder-back chair
- pencil
- drill with wood drill bit
- ruler or measuring tape
- saw
- wooden dowels
- medium-grade sandpaper
- hammer
- royal blue emulsion paint
- medium and fine paintbrushes
- white, fluorescent yellow, green and pink acrylic paints
- permanent black marker
- clear matt varnish

1 Mark the positions of the holes for the dowels. Drill all the holes. Keep the drill straight or the dowel won't pass through both holes.

2 Measure the back of the chair. The dowel should be slightly longer than the chair back.

3 Cut the dowels and sand the ends.

4 Pass the dowel through one upright of the chair and line it up with the hole on the second upright. ⟶

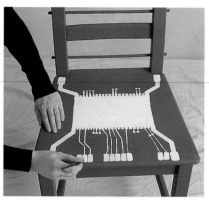

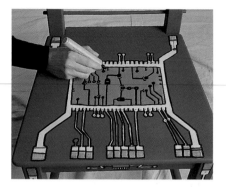

5 With a hammer, lightly tap the dowel through the second hole. Leave an equal amount of dowel showing on either side.

7 With a fine brush and white paint, sketch the outline for the "computer chip" design on the chair seat and on the wide struts of the back. The white provides a good base for the fluorescent paint.

9 With the marker, outline the design. This gives it more impact and you can also add further detail and extra patterns.

6 Paint the whole chair with a blue base coat. Long, slow, even strokes will produce an even finish.

8 Again with a fine brush, paint on the design in yellow, green and pink fluorescent paints.

10 Finally, to protect all the paintwork, coat the whole chair with clear varnish.

SUN LOUNGER

Sun loungers come in various heights and with all kinds of additional features, such as arms and folding sections, but the fabrics, which are mostly garish prints and stripes, seem at odds with the rather smart tubular frames. Apart from the obvious solution of re-covering, using the existing fabric as a pattern, a very smart alternative, which will put an old lounger on a par with design classics of the fifties, is to make a textural webbing cover. This is very hard-wearing, as well as being extremely handsome, and overcomes some of the problems of conventional covers, which often sagged over time, and couldn't be tightened. Re-covered in this way, the lounger offers comfort and durability.

YOU WILL NEED

- ♦ sun lounger
- ♦ chrome cleaner
- ♦ soft cloth
- ♦ measuring tape
- ♦ 2 x 15m/15yd upholstery webbing rolls
- ♦ masking tape
- ♦ pencil
- ♦ scissors
- ♦ 6 packets of large eyelets
- ♦ hammer
- ♦ softwood block
- ♦ needle and matching thread
- ♦ 6m/6yd cord or rope

1 Remove and discard the old cover.

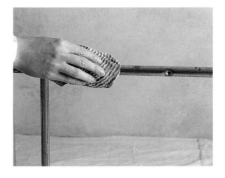

2 Clean the metal frame with chrome cleaner and a soft cloth.

3 Measure the width of the frame for the horizontal straps, and almost double this measurement so that the ends of the straps will nearly meet in the middle. ⟶

4 Position a couple of webbing strips with masking tape and work out how many strips you will need in each section of the frame. Cut the webbing to length and hem the ends.

6 Turning the lounger upside down, wrap the straps round the frame and fasten the ends together with cord or rope where they meet in the middle. Leave a gap wide enough for another

8 Near the hinges, thread another horizontal strap through the vertical ones, but wrap the ends round the two outermost verticals instead of round the frame.

5 Follow the manufacturer's instructions for applying an eyelet to each end of the straps, using a softwood block to protect the floor you are working on.

7 Starting at the foot, secure a vertical strap with an eyelet. Weave the strap under and over the double thickness of the horizontal straps, until you reach the top. Secure the end with another eyelet.

Opposite: Herringbone upholstery webbing in one colour has been used here; it also comes in a natural sand colour, which could be alternated with the grey to create a checkerboard effect.

FUN-FUR CHROME CHAIR

Another common junk-shop find is the chrome-framed chair. This one was in a very bad state – the chrome was spotted with rust and the padding torn. The finished picture shows how even a really tatty chair can be transformed into something smart. The fun-fur covering may seem bizarre but, teamed with the chrome, it turns the chair into a real one-off. You need at least twice the length of each pad.

YOU WILL NEED

- ♦ chrome chair
- ♦ screwdriver
- ♦ chrome cleaner
- ♦ soft cloth
- ♦ craft knife
- ♦ foam or wadding
- ♦ staple gun
- ♦ fun-fur fabric

1 Undo and reserve the screws and remove the old seat pads. Clean the chrome frame with chrome cleaner.

2 Cut away the old covering fabric and padding, to reveal the wooden base of the pads.

3 Cover the base and seat back with new foam or wadding, securing it with a staple gun. Replace the pads.

4 Cover the pads with fun-fur fabric, using a staple gun to attach the fabric to the wood. Take into account the nap of the fabric, so it falls nicely over the curved edge. For the hardest wear, the pile should run from back to front (i.e. it lies flat when smoothed in that direction). Fold the fabric over the chrome supports. Replace the screws.

POLYNESIAN THRONE

A splendid addition to your conservatory or log-cabin-style summer house, this chair festooned with wheat and rushes is not destined to be a mere garden seat, but a haven for sitting and musing. Gardening has become one of the most popular pastimes and garden centres are full of a huge variety of plants and garden paraphernalia. Customized garden furniture is much sought after and pricey, but you can make this stylish throne for very little, with dried grasses, craft brushes, raffia and twigs, which should be available from garden centres or dried-flower shops. Choose a strong, simple chair, preferably with a rush seat. Make your homage to nature. A not-too-serious approach will achieve a chair to be proud of.

YOU WILL NEED

- ◆ wooden chair
- ◆ medium-grade sandpaper
- ◆ oil-based brown paint
- ◆ paintbrush
- ◆ 4 large bunches of wheat
- ◆ 1 large hank of raffia
- ◆ double-sided tape
- ◆ 4 craft rush brushes
- ◆ saw
- ◆ staple gun
- ◆ 4 dried bamboo or rush brushes

1 Sand the wooden surfaces, to provide a key for the paint.

2 Paint the chair with the brown paint to give it a wood-grain effect. You may find it easier to remove the seat.

3 Cover the horizontal strut of the back rest with a few lengths of wheat, tying them in place with raffia. Use the double-sided tape to hold the wheat while you work (the final fixing comes later). Attach two rush brushes diagonally, by binding the stalks to the chair frame and at the crossing point with raffia.

4 Shorten the two remaining rush brushes to the length of the vertical chair struts.

5 To cover the verticals of the back rest, you may find it helpful to bind them loosely with several strands of raffia. Then slot stems of wheat through the raffia until the wood is covered. Do not worry too much about the front of the struts, because two more brushes are tied directly to the front horizontals. Tie the brushes to the verticals.

6 Bind the two side brushes with many twinings of raffia. Discreetly part the brushes and secure them at the top with a few strengthening staples.

7 Add decorative and reinforcing raffia in crisscross fashion to the back of the chair. Knot the raffia to secure it.

8 Choose thin, flexible bamboo or rushes to bend over the top of the legs and staple them in place before binding them with raffia.

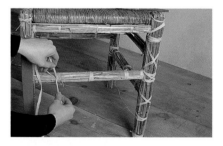

9 Staple a rough covering of wheat and rushes to cover all the legs; don't worry too much about neatness, just cover the surface, and don't overdo the staples because the final raffia binding will do most of the work. As a final touch, and also to make it more long-lasting, knot and crisscross more raffia between your turns.

CHAIR WITH WESTERN FRINGING

If you have an armchair of these robust proportions, it will lend itself to being made over with animal-skin prints and leather fringing. You could also use leatherette for the cushion covers or blankets, which would still be in keeping with this chunky look.

YOU WILL NEED

- ◆ armchair
- ◆ fun-fur or animal-skin fabric
- ◆ upholstery needle and strong thread
- ◆ measuring tape
- ◆ suede or leather
- ◆ self-healing cutting mat
- ◆ ruler
- ◆ craft knife
- ◆ PVA leather glue
- ◆ double-sided tape
- ◆ pencil
- ◆ softwood block
- ◆ studs
- ◆ hammer
- ◆ rubber or softwood scrap

1 Remove the seat cushions and wrap them in fun-fur or animal-skin-print fabric, leaving sufficient fabric to make a continuous flap the length of the cushion. Stitch securely.

2 Using a tape measure, decide on the length of fringing needed to decorate the inside and outside edges of the arms of the chair.

3 Decide how deep you want the fringe on the leather or suede to be. Measure and cut the fringe with a craft knife on a cutting mat, leaving sufficient uncut material to make a hem.

4 Apply PVA glue to the edge of the leather or suede and fold over the hem. Press it down firmly. ⟶

5 Apply double-sided tape to the chair arms.

7 Mark the positions of the studs with a pencil, using a block of wood to gauge the distance between each.

6 Stick the fringing to the tape smoothly. Make sure that it begins and ends at the same place on both arms.

8 Position the studs with your thumb first, press gently and finish with a tap of the hammer, protecting the stud with a rubber or a piece of softwood.

Right: This Western feel has many variations. With the shops full of fun furs and skins and decorative studs, you could make something really wild!

BUCKET STOOL

Florist's buckets in galvanized tin are widely available in a variety of heights; obviously, the taller they are, the better. Cover the seat pad in any fabric (a waffle towel was used here). For a bathroom you could fill PVC or clear plastic with foam chips or fun sponges. Tea towels also make fun covers and a layer of dried lavender would make a lovely scented seat.

YOU WILL NEED

♦ 1m/1yd heavy cord or rope
♦ 2 florist's buckets
♦ glue gun
♦ very large self-cover buttons
♦ scraps of material for covering buttons
♦ fabric-cutting tool for buttons
♦ waffle hand towel
♦ circular cushion pad
♦ large sewing needle
♦ matching thread

1 Attach the cord or rope to the top rim of one of the buckets with the glue gun.

2 Place this bucket inside the second bucket, applying glue to its rim, then invert both buckets.

3 Use the fabric to cover the buttons as per the manufacturer's instructions. The special tool for cutting the fabric is invaluable for this job.

4 Sew the buttons to the centre of the waffle hand towel. Then use the towel to cover the cushion pad. Instead of smoothing out the gathering in the fabric, accentuate it, using the buttons as a focus. Glue the pad to the upturned bucket.

CARDBOARD CHAIR

It's very important that you hunt down cardboard of the heaviest weight from a cardboard manufacturer for this chair. A "treble-skinned" cardboard has been used. Remember that, as with wood, the vertical grain is the strongest. Cardboard is particularly suitable for children, because of their lighter weight. Gum arabic tape is a deceptively strong brown parcel tape.

YOU WILL NEED

- ◆ felt-tipped pen
- ◆ metal ruler
- ◆ 4 sheets of treble-skinned cardboard, 2 x 1.5m/2 x 1¹/₂yd
- ◆ scissors
- ◆ craft knife
- ◆ self-healing cutting mat
- ◆ gum arabic tape
- ◆ 4 thin dowels, pencils or chopsticks, 13cm/5in

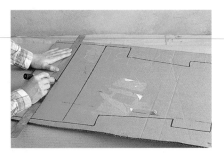

1 Draw the design on to the cardboard, using the diagrams at the back of the book as a guide. Keep the grain of the cardboard running from the top of the chair to the bottom.

2 Using the back of a pair of scissors and the metal ruler, score along the fold lines and, using a craft knife, cut out all the shapes and bind the edges with gum arabic tape.

3 Assemble the chair in the same way as you would make a carton, folding and slotting the cardboard into itself. The back rest of the chair has flaps that fold into the arm rests.

4 Slot the seat into position, making sure it is securely held in place. To give further support, peg pieces of dowel, or even pencils or chopsticks, through the cross-struts.

MATERIALS

The materials and equipment used in these projects are quite wide-ranging. For the basic stripping down and making good of an old chair, before adding the new decoration, you will need wadding or herringbone upholstery webbing for the seat, which are both widely available. Wooden surfaces benefit from being sanded down with medium-grade sandpaper to provide a good key for the new paint. If you want to remove an old layer of paint, use paint stripper, but it is essential to wear full protective clothing and to follow the manufacturer's instructions.

There are two main types of paint, water-based and oil-based. Wherever possible, water-based paints have been specified for the projects. These paints can be thinned with water. You may, however, prefer to use oil-based paints. Oil-based and water-based paints are not compatible and should not be mixed. With all paints, allow each coat to dry thoroughly before applying successive coats. Varnishes are used to protect paintwork from general wear and tear. As with paints, varnishes come

in both oil- and water-based varieties and in matt, satin or gloss finishes. When applying varnish, use a clean brush that has not been used for paint.

Your basic tool kit should include a glue gun, a staple gun, a measuring tape, a sewing machine, a pair of pliers and a hammer. A craft knife with a set of blades is essential. If you feel that you would get enough use out of it, buy an eyelet punch, or alternatively, you can buy cheaper eyelet packs with disposable tools.

Always keep your eyes open for interesting materials that might be useful for covering chairs, or using as throws. Gather together a good collection of buttons, braids, string and general bits and pieces. This way you will avoid the hassle of having to start from scratch each time you want to decorate a chair.

Staple gun (1); measuring tape (2); scissors (3); eyelets and poppers (4); herringbone upholstery tape (5); self-cover buttons (6); tacking thread (7); cotton thread (8); translucent fabric (9).

TECHNIQUES

Covering a seat pad

Often chairs need little more than a new cover, a replacement seat or a coat of paint to make them as good as new. Here are a few basic techniques for renovating old chairs.

1 Remove all of the old, stained or damaged material. Using the seat pad as a template, cut a piece of fabric just large enough to cover the underside of the pad.

2 Check to see that the structure of the pad is sound. If it is sagging, bolster it with more wadding felt. To give the pad a smooth, rounded shape, cover the whole pad in a thin layer of wadding, fixing this to the underside of the pad with a staple gun.

3 Allow sufficient width and depth of new seat-covering fabric to cover the top and sides of the pad, plus a generous allowance for folding to the underside. Cut out the cover.

4 Put the fabric evenly in position over the pad, stretch it to hand-tightness and secure it initially with a staple on each of the four sides.

5 Staple at intervals of about 2.5cm/ 1in, pulling the corners taut and, if the fabric is thick, forming an envelope corner. Turn the edges in and press them flat. Staple or slip-stitch the underneath piece in place.

Replacing damaged webbing on an old seat

1 Remove all damaged webbing and old tacks. Measure and cut strips of new herringbone upholstery webbing, using the old strips as a guide.

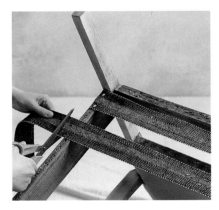

2 Position the cross strips, stretch them taut and secure them with upholstery tacks.

3 Tack the front-to-back strips in position at the back and weave them under and over the cross strips, until you reach the front edge of the seat frame. Pull them taut and fasten them with upholstery tacks.

Fitting a new wooden seat

1 Remove the old damaged seat with a craft knife, pincers or screwdriver.

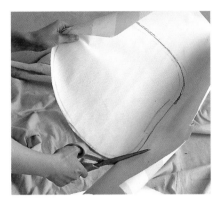

2 If possible, use the old seat as a template. If not, make a paper template, as explained in the instructions for the Gilded Chair.

3 Cut out the new seat with a jigsaw or take the template to a timber merchant or DIY store to be cut for you. Sand the edges. To fix the seat in place, pin it with panel pins. The heads can be sunk with a nail punch.

Stripping and sanding

Many old chairs benefit from being stripped back and sanded. This should be done wearing strong gloves and old clothes. Apply chemical paint stripper with a brush, to all surfaces. Leave for 5 minutes (or as directed by the manufacturer) and wash off with warm, soapy water and wire wool. Repeat until you have removed all the paint and varnish. For best results, sand the chair with three grades of sandpaper, starting with a coarse grade, moving on to a medium grade and ending with a fine grade. Always sand in the direction of the wood grain. On flat surfaces, use a sanding block that allows you to apply greater pressure more evenly. Wrap sandpaper around a piece of dowel for any inside curves or places that are difficult to reach. The chair is now ready for a new finish such as painting or waxing.

Sealing and waxing

Once a wooden chair or stool has been sanded down, sealing and waxing it will make the wood glow softly, which is more appealing than the hard shine produced by varnishing. It doesn't give much protection against marks but, if you keep rewaxing every three to six months, a natural patina will build up.

1 Simply brush the sealant on with a paintbrush. You may need two coats. Leave to dry.

2 Many different coloured waxes are available but they are all applied in the same way. Rub generous amounts of wax into all the surfaces of the chair with wire wool.

3 Buff up with a clean, soft cloth.

T E M P L A T E S

Dining chair with laces

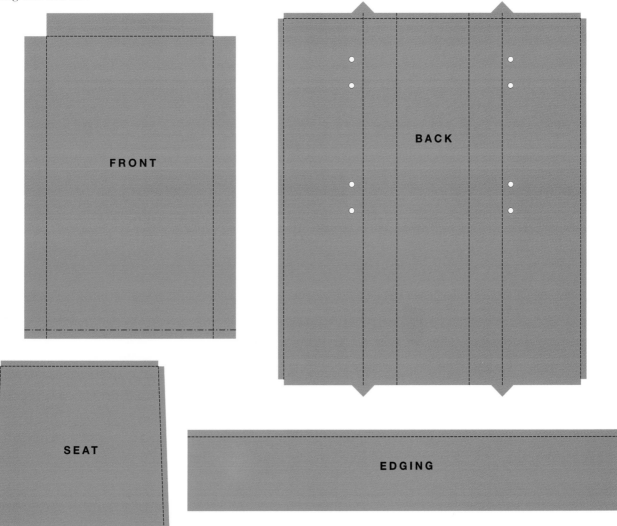

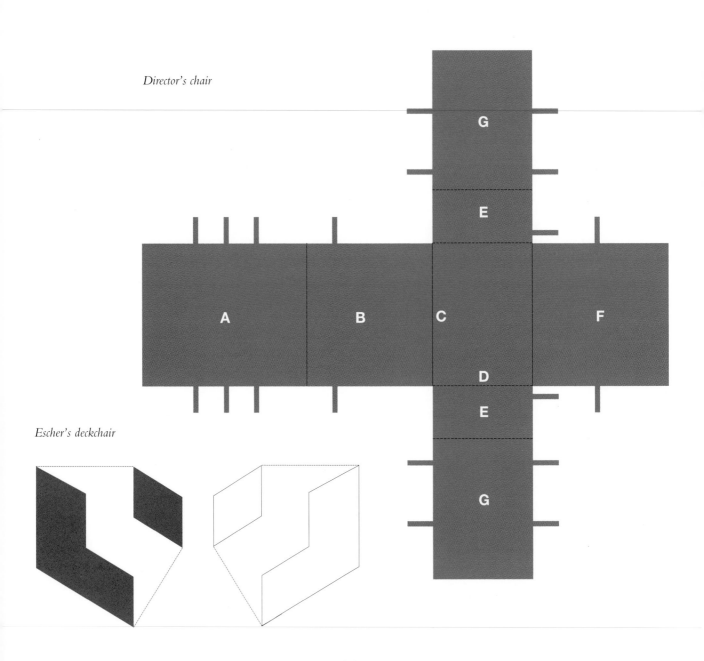

Director's chair

G

E

A   B   C   F

D

E

G

Escher's deckchair

CHAIR SEAT

Cardboard chair

LOOSE CHAIR BACK

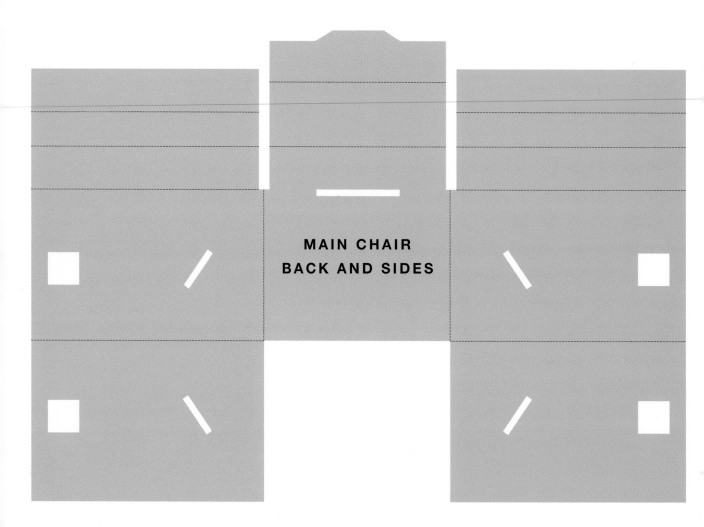

MAIN CHAIR
BACK AND SIDES

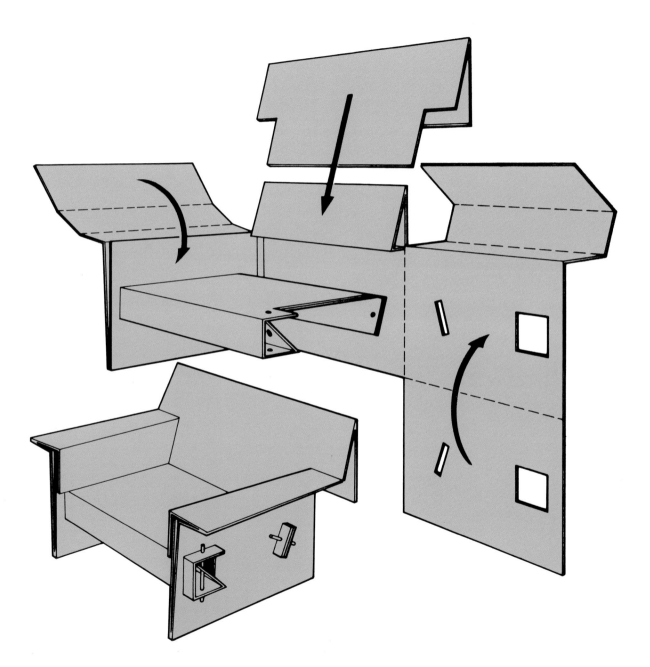

INDEX

Acknowledgments
The author and publishers
would like to thank After
Noah in London for their
generosity in supplying
furniture and galvanized
accessories and Crown
Decorative Products Ltd.
Darwin, Lancashire, England
for their generosity in
supplying paint.